HOW TO R[...] YOUR VIRGINITY

. . .and 99 Other Recent Discoveries About Sex.

by Patricia Marx
and Charlotte Stuart

Workman Publishing
New York

To Charlie.

Library of Congress Cataloging in Publication Data

Marx, Patricia.
   How to regain your virginity, and 99 other recent
discoveries about sex.
   1. Sex—Anecdotes, facetiae, satire, etc. I. Stuart,
Charlotte. II. Title.
PN6231.M54M37   1983   818'.5402'08   83-1341
ISBN 0-89480-365-4

Cover and book design by Douglass Grimmett
Illustrations by Philip A. Scheuer
Original photography by Robin Holland
Cover illustration by Dan Kirk

Workman Publishing Company, Inc.
1 West 39th Street
New York, New York 10018
Manufactured in the United States
First printing May 1983
10 9 8 7 6 5 4 3 2 1

Acknowledgments

We'd like to thank our wonderful editor Sally Kovalchick, whose wit and judgment made this book possible, and our talented art director Doug Grimmett, whose visions made our ideas much funnier. We'd also like to thank our patrons, Charlie Stuart and Janice and Richard Marx, who paid a lot of money for this book.

Thanks also to the following virgins: Alison Ashley, Rona Beame, Blair Brown, Gwen Cassel, Susan Connor, Julia Cooper-Smith, Sarah Crichton, Mark Falls, Louise Gikow, Jane Grimmett, Douglass Grimmett, Alexandra Halsey, Guy Martin, Doug McGrath, Lug McGrath, Julienne McNeer, Hilary Meserole, Lawrence F. O'Donnell, Mark O'Donnell, Steven O'Donnell, Abigail Owen, Wendy Palitz, Jacqueline Payne, William Payne, Pat Pendleton, Chris Power, Rockey Rakita, Eric Rayman, Riverrun, Jennifer Rogers, Joy Rose, Victoria Rostow, Rebecca Sangster, Ludwig Tomazic, Jimmy Warner, Priscilla Warner, Liz Welch, Jacques Williams, and William Winslow.

Preface

Studies show that the more people read about sex, the more confused they become. Therefore, this book was product-tested in Atlanta, Georgia, and it was found to actually lessen confusion about sex.

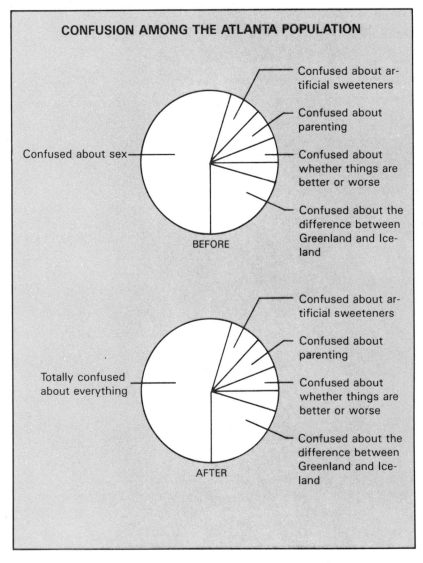

CONFUSION AMONG THE ATLANTA POPULATION

Confused about sex

Confused about artificial sweeteners

Confused about parenting

Confused about whether things are better or worse

Confused about the difference between Greenland and Iceland

BEFORE

Totally confused about everything

Confused about artificial sweeteners

Confused about parenting

Confused about whether things are better or worse

Confused about the difference between Greenland and Iceland

AFTER

CONTENTS

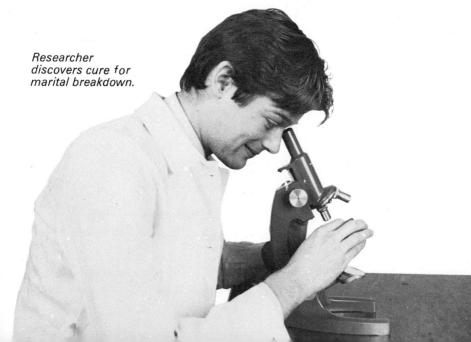

*Researcher
discovers cure for
marital breakdown.*

*Two famous
sexologists
are stumped.*

Foreword

This volume does not promise to be anything more than what it is: the most comprehensive study of human sexuality to date. Many of the theories presented here are bold and daring. Some probably will not be accepted by the scientific community, or even by the general public. But we caution the reader not to reject our theses outright. We ask only that the book be read carefully, that each fact be weighed and each argument examined. We hope that the data presented will allay the sexual frustrations of millions of men and women and bring an educated intelligence into a field where prejudice and speculation have prevailed too long. But if our book does nothing more than stimulate informed public discussions about human sexuality, we will have succeeded.

1. HOW TO REGAIN YOUR VIRGINITY.

This is not a crash program. This is not a fad. Our five-day "How to Regain Your Virginity" program is scientifically proven. But we must warn you—it's tough. You must make a commitment to the program. Read each exercise. Twice! Learn them step by step. Memorize them. Never say, "I can't." You *can.* We will show you how.

Before you begin, be sure to consult your physician.

Before regaining virginity

After regaining virginity

DAY 1

Go out and have a good time! You may never have one again.

DAY 2

Day 2 is Behavior Modification Day. By the end of today, you may not have *become* a virgin, but you will *behave* like one. And, after all, virginity is 25 percent behavior. *

Behavior modification is based on the theories of the Russian physiologist Ivan Petrovich Pavlov, who taught his dog how to ring a bell when he (the dog) was hungry. The process is a simple one of learning by doing, and is based on reward and punishment.

A nonvirgin drives with her foot on the floor and her hand on the horn.

A virgin wears a seatbelt when she moves the car in the driveway.

The actual breakdown of virginity: 25 percent behavior, 40 percent physical appearance, 25 percent mental state, and 10 percent legal status.

Here's how to break your old habits and permanently alter your lifestyle:

OLD NONVIRGIN HABITS *Each time you slip into one of these, apply 500 volts of current to your forearm.*	NEW VIRGIN HABITS *Each time you try one of these, reward yourself with a dog biscuit.*
Speaking loudly	Speaking so softly that no one has any idea what you're saying
Establishing eye contact when you talk to a member of the opposite sex	Looking down bashfully when a member of the opposite sex walks by
Writing your telephone number on the subway seat	Writing a poem about the coming of spring
Singing "Twist and Shout" in the shower	Humming "Put on a Happy Face" as you bathe
Chewing gum	Chewing your food a hundred times before you swallow
Inviting someone over for a Harvey's Bristol Cream	Never having heard of Harvey's Bristol Cream
Driving with your foot on the floor and your hand on the horn	Wearing a seatbelt when you move the car in the driveway
Going out boogying	Staying home and listening to a PBS simulcast of the *Nutcracker Suite*
Keeping a man's bathrobe in your closet (if you're a woman)	Never having wondered what men wear to bed
Asking the guy sleeping next to you to turn off the alarm in the morning	Jumping right out of bed when the alarm rings and splashing your face with cold water

DAY 3

Eat grapefruits all day. This usually does not work, but it is worth a try.

DAY 4

Prepare for Mental Virgination. Derived from an ancient Hindu formula that was lost for centuries and was only recently rediscovered by the authors of this book, this treatment promises to leave you as innocent as a lamb.

7 A.M.: To rid your mind of all unclean thoughts that accumulated overnight, vacuum out your head with a good, sturdy rug attachment.

Midmorning: A time when many are tempted to go off their Clean Thought Regimen. Don't let this happen to you! Hang by your feet, shaking your head vigorously for a half hour to shake out mental germs.

3 P.M.: Drive to the airport, where there are wonderful machines that detect, as if by X-ray, any dirty thoughts that may lurk in your mind. If your head isn't absolutely empty, ask the guard if you can borrow his bludgeon and give your head a good whack.

8 P.M.: Time for bed! But tonight you will be wearing your new Thought Pasteurization Earmuffs, which destroy disease-producing bacteria in your mind by heating your ears up to 145 degrees Fahrenheit. Clean dreams!

DAY 5

Now that you have learned the ways of a virgin and your thoughts are clean, it is time for you to move forward and become acquainted with the Virgin Creed.

Recite the Creed slowly, thinking about what you are saying.

The Virgin Creed

A Virgin believes in being friendly but not too friendly.

A Virgin believes in being clean in thought, word, and especially deed.

A Virgin believes in letting her conscience be her guide and never seeking help from consenting adults.

A Virgin believes that a good time the night before will bring a mourning after.

A Virgin believes that a reproductive organ is not as good as the original.

A Virgin believes in docu-dramas but not in fantasies.

A Virgin believes in marriage as long as she and her husband are "just friends."

A Virgin believes she is a kite sailing in the sky on a cloudless day in May.

And more.

Congratulations! You are now an official virgin.

Virginity Progress Chart

DAY 1

My teeth are whiter.

Some one told a dirty joke and I didn't get it.

There is a song in my heart.

My nails are stronger.

DAY 2

I run faster and jump higher.

There is a bounce to my step.

I blushed today when someone told me it was snowing down south.

DAY 3

My skin glows.

My crow's-feet have vanished.

I feel foot-loose and fancy free.

DAY 4

The natural highlights in my hair came out today.

The bloom is back on the rose.

I can't believe Salinger uses the word *damn* in *The Catcher in the Rye*!

DAY 5

The hills are alive with the sound of music.

Babies are found under cabbages, aren't they?

I'm a virgin!

2. A VIRGINITY MAINTENANCE PROGRAM.

There is no point in regaining your virginity if you don't take care of it. Experts agree there are two ways to keep your virginity.

1. Put it in the refrigerator. It will keep for weeks.
2. Lock yourself up in a closet. But first check to see that no one else is there.

Whichever program you choose, remember that maintaining your virginity is a way of life. Here are a few tips:

▶ The hardest place to maintain your virginity is at a party. Explain to your host or hostess about the "new you." He or she will be more than happy to accommodate your new needs—and may even want to become a virgin, too.

▶ If your old friends or spouse say you're not any fun anymore and urge you to "cheat a little," get rid of 'em! They weren't your friends in the first place!

▶ Avoid salty foods.

▶ Don't be discouraged if you find others unreceptive to regaining their virginity. The world doesn't change overnight. And remember, *you* can't make others want to regain their virginity. *They* must want to.

▶ If you find yourself weakening, don't try to be a hero! Call the Virginity Hotline (1-800-555-3950). There's a virgin there to listen twenty-four hours a day.

3. NEW EVIDENCE INDICATES THE SEXUAL REVOLUTION PRECEDED THE BRONZE AGE.

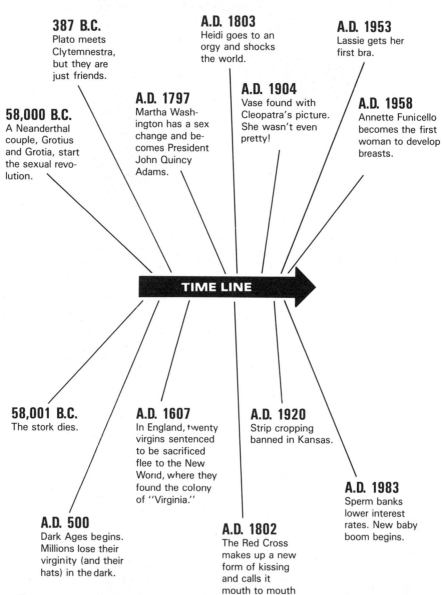

387 B.C.
Plato meets Clytemnestra, but they are just friends.

A.D. 1803
Heidi goes to an orgy and shocks the world.

A.D. 1953
Lassie gets her first bra.

A.D. 1797
Martha Washington has a sex change and becomes President John Quincy Adams.

A.D. 1904
Vase found with Cleopatra's picture. She wasn't even pretty!

A.D. 1958
Annette Funicello becomes the first woman to develop breasts.

58,000 B.C.
A Neanderthal couple, Grotius and Grotia, start the sexual revolution.

TIME LINE

58,001 B.C.
The stork dies.

A.D. 1607
In England, twenty virgins sentenced to be sacrificed flee to the New World, where they found the colony of "Virginia."

A.D. 1920
Strip cropping banned in Kansas.

A.D. 500
Dark Ages begins. Millions lose their virginity (and their hats) in the dark.

A.D. 1802
The Red Cross makes up a new form of kissing and calls it mouth to mouth resuscitation.

A.D. 1983
Sperm banks lower interest rates. New baby boom begins.

4. DO YOU HAVE A DIRTY MIND?

A Scientific Test

Here's a fun crossword puzzle.

Do you have a pencil?

Across

2. A man and a woman are of the opposite____.

3. Simone de Beauvoir wrote a book called *The Second*____.

4. ____without love is immoral.

5. A word that rhymes with Tex and starts with an *s* is ____.

Down

1. Raquel Welch is very ____y.

2. Women are often called "the fair____."

3. One of six offspring born at a single birth is called a ____tuplet.

4. All I ever think about is ____.

Correct answers if you have a dirty mind.

Correct answers if you have a clean mind.

5. IRANIAN SEX CODE CRACKED.

Any youth hosteler can tell you a tale or two about the time he asked for a cup of coffee in Teheran and ended up with a sex change operation—and a cup of tea! The subtleties of the Iranian language of love have eluded linguists for years. Fortunately, a Rosetta-like stone has recently been discovered, making the language accessible to all.

In Iran . . .

▶ The word for *sex* is the same as the word for *air conditioner.*

▶ There are over seventeen words for *voyeurism.*

▶ The present perfect tense is used only by people who are on intimate terms.

▶ If you put the accent on the last syllable while you are ordering at a restaurant, it means you wish to purchase a sex gadget and will pay any price for it.

▶ There is a tribe in the marshlands of Hamun-e Helmand that uses only dirty words.

6. MORE PEOPLE HAVE HAD SEX PROBLEMS THAN HAVE HAD SEX.

Radio psychologists find the following are the most common sex problems among their listeners:

1. If it takes one woman nine months to have a baby, how long would it take four women to have one baby?

2. Sue, Tom, and Dave are friends. Sue, who used to go out with Dave, thinks Tom is a: but likes him to some degree, say 30 degrees, whereas Dave likes Sue 40 degrees. What is the chance their love triangle is isosceles?

3. If all the books written about sex were lined up end to end, how many times would they circle the earth?

4. $(NH_4)_2SO_4$ is the formula for what common aphrodisiac?

5. What was the birth rate in the Fertile Crescent?

Two famous sexologists stumped.

7. NEW THEORY OF EVOLUTION.

No, I insist. You go first.

8. PANEL EXPOSES TWENTY WORDS AS "ALMOST DIRTY."

The Congressional Panel on Obscenity suggests that the following words be used with parental guidance:

rapier	fallacious	screwdriver
adulterate	penal	luster
cockatoo	titular	erroneous
consommé	spurn	combustible
sects	capitulate	laity
masticate	dickey	hot cross buns
Balzac	crotchety	

9. THERE *IS* SEX BEFORE LIFE.

In-depth interviews and observational studies of more than 120 human fetuses suggest that Sigmund Freud's ''sex drive'' exists prenatally and, moreover, that a newborn baby is not necessarily a virgin.

THE GROWTH OF A FETUS

ONE (1) MONTH
The brain, spinal cord, and nervous system are established. A premature face is forming, including eyes, ears, and mouth, but, by and large, it is all a mess.

TWO (2) MONTHS
The digestive system is well-developed, and already the fetus has acquired a taste for some of the milder cheeses.

THREE (3) MONTHS
The fetus is aware of its own name and is curious about the world around it. It shows a keen interest in the lives of the nearby kidneys and large intestine.

FOUR (4) MONTHS
The fetus is becoming more independent of the mother. Often it will refuse to keep the same hours as the mother, or to hold the same political views. Also, the fetus develops wings, which will disappear by the sixth month.

FIVE (5) MONTHS
The fetus measures ten inches long and is getting sick and tired of standing on its head.

SIX (6) MONTHS
The fetus decides to take up Spanish in its spare time. It sends away for language tapes and books.

SEVEN (7) MONTHS
The fetus is capable of having sex but decides against it.

EIGHT (8) MONTHS
The fetus takes a vacation.

**CHILDBIRTH
NINE (9) MONTHS**
The fetus starts to plan for the future. It considers money market funds, but wants something less risky at this stage.

10. MOST SEX OCCURS WITHIN A FIFTEEN-MILE RADIUS OF THE HOME.

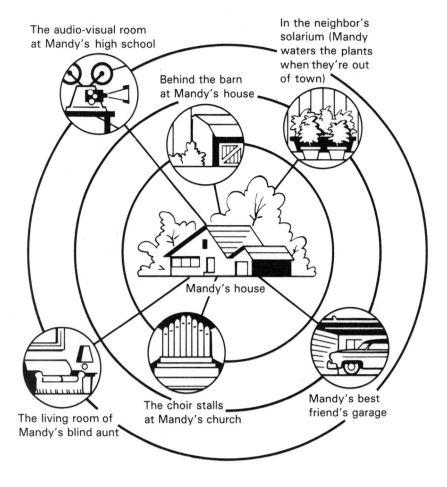

The audio-visual room at Mandy's high school

Behind the barn at Mandy's house

In the neighbor's solarium (Mandy waters the plants when they're out of town)

Mandy's house

The living room of Mandy's blind aunt

The choir stalls at Mandy's church

Mandy's best friend's garage

11. WHAT TO TELL YOUR PARENTS ABOUT SEX.
Dr. Spock's Theories Overturned

Should I allow my parents to sleep in the same bed together?
People are people. Sexual feelings are bound to occur between two people who regularly share the same bed. So, if possible, don't allow Mom and Dad to sleep in the same bedroom.

Should I show my parents examples of sex in nature?
If your parents are old enough to ask the questions, they're old enough to learn the truth. There's no better way to teach your parents about sex than to cite the examples of our friends in the animal kingdom.

At what age should I tell my parents the facts of life?
As soon as you reach puberty.

How late should I let my parents stay out?
Your parents should be in by nine o'clock on workdays. After all, they have to be up early the next morning. Who's going to iron your pants? Who's going to go out and earn the daily bread?

Should I allow my parents to go steady?
Parents who need to go steady are usually very insecure. They can't cope with the pressures of dating a variety of people or they feel they have to conform to what's "in." Tell your parents it's O.K. that they maintain a special affection toward each other, but urge that they see other parents.

Should I allow my parents to see me nude?
There are children who feel it's very important to walk around nude in front of their parents, but in some cases, this can traumatize the parent and lead to an unhappy attitude toward sex. Explain to your parents that you love them very much but you feel you should respect each others' privacy.

What if my parents never ask questions about sex?
It is unusual for a parent to reach the age of thirty-five without expressing some curiosity about sex. If your parents never ask questions when, for instance, they see a pregnant woman or a baby being diapered, they probably got the feeling at home that such questions were "off limits." Perhaps you should try to think of ways to introduce the subject yourself. Why not arrange to have a neighbor come over and bathe a baby in your home. Or point to a pregnant woman and say, "I guess she's been having intercourse."

12. NEW SEX EXPERIMENTS YOU CAN DO AT HOME.

An Experiment

▶ What you need:

1. Different kinds of food such as oranges, apples, lemons, and tomatoes.

2. An MX missile. (If you don't have an MX missile, ask Mom if you can borow a knife from the kitchen. But be careful! A knife is not a toy!)

▶ What you do:

1. Take off your clothes.

2. Cut off a piece from each food.

3. Make a chart to show which foods are red and which are not.

▶ What you find:

Foods	Red	Not red
oranges		X
apples (with skin)	X	
lemons		X
tomatoes	X	

▶ Why:

No one knows.

Another Experiment

▶ Do this:

Amusing Recombinant DNA.

1. Take an old shoe box.
2. Poke holes in one end of the shoe box with a pencil.
3. Put dirt in the shoe box.
4. Take off your clothes.

▶ What did you learn? Did you have an orgasm?

_____

_____

_____

13. THE AMOEBA IS THE LITTLEST ORGASM IN THE WHOLE WORLD.

The amoeba (also "ameba"), a microscopic, one-celled animal that lives in stagnant waters or off others as a parasite, is so little it has to have special clothes made for it.

The parasitic amoeba crashes a swim party.

14. TWO OUT OF THREE CASES OF LOST VIRGINITY ARE NEVER REPORTED.

Is it unemployment, television, or the deterioration of the nuclear family that is causing virginity-related crimes to reach epidemic proportions? "It is definitely one of those things or it is none of them," comments Officer Lamston of the Police Commission on Crime.

According to the latest Police Index on Crime:

▶ More people lose their virginity than their wallets.

▶ More people lose their virginity per month in New York City than died in the Korean War.

▶ 2 percent of the people who lose their virginity have it returned in the mail.

▶ 24 percent of the people who report cases of stolen virginity are lying. They are only after the insurance.

▶ On the black market, virginity sometimes goes for as much as $1,500.

▶ Police throw out more than 20,000 cases of unclaimed virginity annually. (More than 30,000 cases are donated to orphanages and hospitals.)

15. WHAT TO DO IF YOU'VE LOST YOUR VIRGINITY AND CAN'T GET TO A PHONE TO REPORT IT.

Officer Lamston's Guidelines:

1. Make sure you have really lost it and not just misplaced it. Take a good look around. Are you wearing it?
2. Wrap yourself in a blanket and roll around on the floor.
3. Do not operate heavy machinery.
4. Stay calm. Maybe your virginity wasn't worth that much in the first place.

16. HOW BABIES ARE MADE.

When a penny is inserted into the baby machine, a baby is pushed through the system. Contrary to popular belief, it is just a matter of chance whether you get a boy or a girl or a lucky key chain.

17. WHEN HORSES GO ON DATES, THE GIRL HORSE ALWAYS PAYS.

Horses neck 'n' neck.

18. THE BABY VIRGIN.

Infants Fed Exclusively on Soy Milk Formula Never Reach Adultery

HOW TO BECOME THE BABY VIRGIN

1. Whenever you and someone else say the same word at the same time, shout, *"Jinx you one-two-three-four-five-six-seven-eight-nine-ten owe me a Coke!"*
2. Eat only the cream filling of Oreos.
3. If you're attracted to a guy and you see him walking down the street, walk on the opposite side.
4. Memorize the lyrics to all the TV theme songs.
5. As soon as your date drops you off, rush inside, call up everyone you know, and tell them everything that happened.
6. Skip everywhere.

Virgin Type A

19. HOW TO TELL IF YOUR LOVER HAS PASSED AWAY.

1. When we make love, my lover:
    a. does something else.
    b. is not there.
    c. sings camp songs.
    d. does not help.
    e. is stiff as a board.

2. When we go to parties, my lover:
    a. is the only one whose skin is decomposed.
    b. remains in his/her coffin.
    c. must wear cellophane.
    d. always brings a tennis racket.
    e. must be stuffed with cotton.

3. When I put a mirror up to my lover's mouth, I see:
    a. breath on the mirror.
    b. no breath on the mirror.
    c. that I am going to have bad luck for seven years.
    d. that I have made a mistake choosing my lover.
    e. green.

4. What I like most about my lover is:
    a. the inscription on his/her tombstone.
    b. his/her silence.
    c. nothing to brag about.
    d. his/her best friend.

Solution: There is no solution. Death is final.

20. ARCHAEOLOGISTS UNCOVER LOST SEX CIVILIZATION.

Archaeologists excavating a site at Big Sur, California, have unearthed artifacts dating as far back as 1962 that prove conclusively that civilization in that era was centered around sex.

Archaeologists agree that this artifact was definitely a sex device or perhaps a contraceptive.

The decrease in sexual activity among women today alarms geologists, who predict the trend will drastically alter the earth's climate.

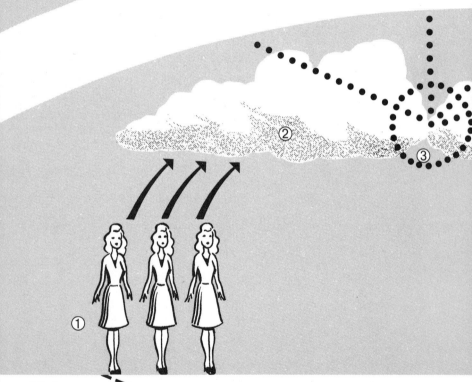

OZONE LAYER

(1) As more and more women become frigid, they cool the earth's atmosphere, pushing the warm air upward.
(2) The rising warm air is cooled to its dew point and clouds are formed.
(3) As more and more clouds form, they collide (4), sparking off

ions that penetrate the ozone layer. Eventually the ozone layer disintegrates and (5) the earth becomes exposed to the sun's radiation. (6) Vegetation drops off. The soil becomes loosened and (7) the earth caves in.

CONTINUED ▶

Meanwhile...

(8) The sun's radiation melts sheets of ice at the North Pole. These break off and slide into the great valleys of the earth, creating a new Ice Age.

The Ice Age lasts until women become more responsive again, at which point the entire process is reversed.

22. HALF THE WORLD'S STERILE COTTON COMES FROM THE VIRGIN ISLANDS.

More than two million virgins visit the Virgin Islands each year. They come to enjoy the sandy beaches, the fishing, the hotels, restaurants, bargain shopping, and, of course, the famous castles and forts built by pirates.

But what you may not know is that the Virgin Islands is not only just a popular resort for virgins. In fact, nearly half its gross national income is derived from agriculture.

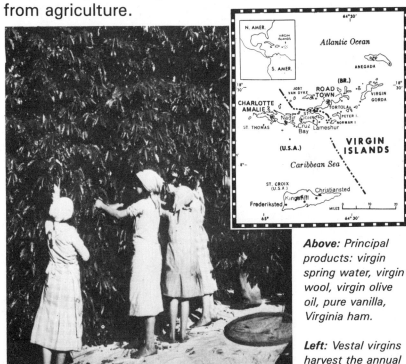

Above: Principal products: virgin spring water, virgin wool, virgin olive oil, pure vanilla, Virginia ham.

Left: Vestal virgins harvest the annual Ivory Soap crop (99.44 percent pure).

23. MASTERS AND JOHNSON BEGAN AS A ONE-NIGHT STAND.

In the Depression, when times were tough, Masters and Johnson had an idea.

ONE NIGHT ONLY-5¢

Today that idea has blossomed into a multimillion-dollar sex clinic franchise. You can always tell a Masters and Johnson Sex Clinic by the orange roof!

24. THE LITE SEX REPORT: A NATIONWIDE STUDY OF MALE AND FEMALE NONSEXUALITY

Freud, Kinsey, Masters and Johnson, Comfort — they all had one thing on their minds: s-e-x. But women or men have never been asked what they've felt about *not* having sex.

How many times a week do they not have sex? Do they ever think about not having sex with another partner? How do they feel about not having sex with a married man or woman? What kind of fantasies do they have that do not involve sex? What nonsexual activity gives them the most pleasure?

Hitherto, these questions have been unasked and consequently unanswered. Now, for the first time, we let the women and men of America speak for themselves about their nonsexual feelings. Our questionnaire was sent to over seven virgins nationwide.

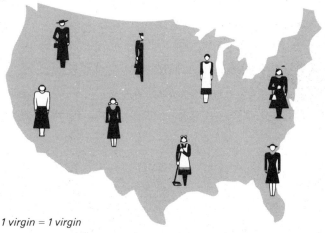

1 virgin = 1 virgin

25. THE LITE SEX REPORT SEX QUESTIONNAIRE.

Below is a copy of the Lite Sex Questionnaire we sent to over seven virgins nationwide. In the interest of continuing research, please fill it out and return it to: Lite Questionnaire, Grand Central Station, New York, N.Y.

1. How old were you when you first did not have sex?
   20 years young. . . . . ☐
   Older than you think . . . . ☐
   As old as the night is young . . . . ☐
   Younger than springtime . . . . ☐

2. How would you describe your first nonsexual activity?
   Like eating a double-dip chocolate chocolate chip
      ice-cream cone . . . . ☐
   Great, except I got too sunburned . . . . ☐
   Y'know, like, um, I mean like really wow . . . . ☐
   None of your business . . . . ☐

3. I prefer no sex because:
   There is no physical contact . . . . ☐
   You don't have to worry about what to name the baby . ☐
   I have many allergies. . . . . ☐
   It is sodium-free!. . . . . ☐

4. I believe the sexual revolution has
   Replaced workers with automated machines . . . . ☐
   Been made into a movie . . . . ☐
   Not given me enough credit. ☐
   A lot to learn . . . . ☐

5. In your own words, trace the origins and development of the Renaissance._____
   _____
   _____

26. THE LITE SEX REPORT: MOST WOMEN WHO EXPERIENCED VIRGINITY DID SHOW PHYSICAL SIGNS.

It has often been said that if you have to ask what virginity is, you've never experienced it. About half the women who answered the Lite Sex Survey had experienced virginity and were most candid and articulate about what it felt like:

"I never felt like a whole woman until I experienced virginity for the first time."

—A forty-year-old housewife from Illinois

"No more headaches for me! I go to sleep every night right off the bat and wake up every morning bright and alert and ready to face the world without a crutch. Even my husband has noticed."

—A thirty-two-year-old telecommunications analyst from Missouri

"I feel tender and loving and want to be close."

—An eleven-year-old ice-skater from Ohio

"I don't know. I think virginity was kind of a disappointment, personally."

—A thirty-one-year-old swinger from Florida

"It's kind of nice. It's like the feeling you get when you're in a long line at the bank on a Friday and the dry cleaning place is about to close and the girl in front of you gets out of line. You feel really good and warm all over."

—A twenty-year-old college student and caterer from New York

"Wow! I feel like my brain is being lobotomized by small electric shock waves."

—A twenty-seven-year-old social studies teacher from Massachusetts

"I read a lot about it and heard other women talk about it, but I never thought it could happen to me."

—A forty-two-year-old fashion designer from New Jersey

27. TWO-THIRDS OF ALL MEN IN THE LITE SEX SURVEY EXPRESSED POSITIVE VIEWS ABOUT WOMEN WHO HAVE REGAINED THEIR VIRGINITY.

We've all heard the warnings of social scientists that the new virgins threaten the very fiber of society's existence. Not only do men supposedly detest this new female breed; they are violently afraid of it. To the contrary, report the men who answered *the Lite Sex Survey:*

"Once the sex issue is removed, it's so much easier to go to bed with somebody."

—A fifty-three-year-old garage mechanic from Pennsylvania

"I don't feel that today's virgins are any different. They have just been allowed to express publicly and openly the emotions and opinions they have had for generations. Right on, virgins!"

—The twenty-five-year-old president of "Gay Virgins of Chicago"

"Wonderful wives and mothers. No doubt about it."

—A twenty-two-year-old student from Colorado

"Today's women are nicer and better than ever. They were always good but the virgins now are much better. They are more stimulating, both intellectually and otherwise. They are more self-reliant, etc. As far as I am concerned, virgins are the tops. Of course, I'd never go out with one.

—A forty-four-year-old dentist from Maryland

28. THE ROMANTIC VIRGIN.

How to Save Yourself for the Right Man and Dominate the Sex Futures Market

HOW TO BECOME THE ROMANTIC VIRGIN

1. Write bad poetry about your feelings while listening to Bob Dylan's "Just Like a Woman."

2. Burst into uncontrollable tears when Bambi's mother dies.

3. Fall madly in love with someone you've never met (preferably Darcy from *Pride and Prejudice*).

4. Break up dramatically with someone you've never gone out with (preferably Wickham from *Pride and Prejudice*).

5. Kiss a frog.

Virgin Type B

29. PARTS OF THE UTERUS DECLASSIFIED.

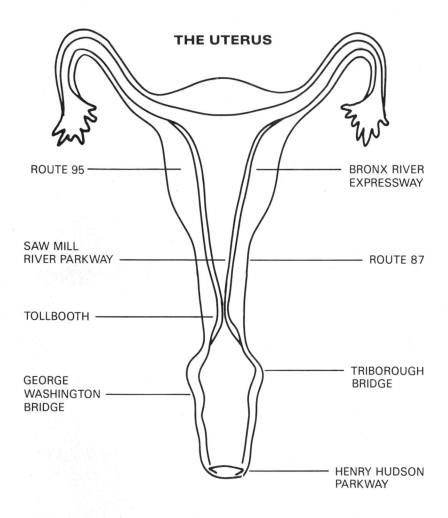

THE UTERUS

ROUTE 95

BRONX RIVER
EXPRESSWAY

SAW MILL
RIVER PARKWAY

ROUTE 87

TOLLBOOTH

GEORGE
WASHINGTON
BRIDGE

TRIBOROUGH
BRIDGE

HENRY HUDSON
PARKWAY

To the Triborough: take Route 95 to the Saw Mill South and follow that until Route 87 (after the toll); follow 87, which will take you to the Triborough. Look for signs.

30. 1983 TEST-TUBE BABIES.
A Miracle of Modern Engineering

Genetic engineers at General Baby have developed a new process involving recombinant DNA that enables them to mass-produce test-tube babies of a quality comparable to custom-made ones. Says General Baby President Brad Gunther: ''Our 1983 test-tube babies rival any foreign imports on the market today. But go ahead: if you can find a better baby, buy it.''

A proud father sees his baby for the first time. Somehow a father always knows which baby is his.

31. HOW TO BECOME A SEXOLOGIST.

You can! Two-thirds of all high school graduates are turning to sexology as a stimulating and fun way to make money.

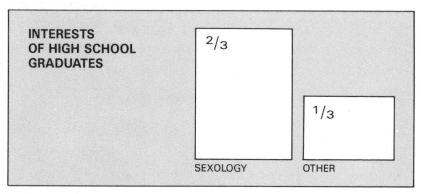

INTERESTS
OF HIGH SCHOOL
GRADUATES

2/3

1/3

SEXOLOGY   OTHER

But how do you start? Let's follow Kevin as he makes his way from being an anonymous student to being a famous sexologist.

First Kevin visits the high school guidance counselor, Mr. Rorison, to "rap" about his continuing educational goals. They decide that sexology is where his head's at.

So Kevin marches off to the American Sexology Institute at Akron, where he meets boys and girls with similar interests.
In the lab, Kevin and his classmates discover the cure for marital breakdown. At the end of his second year, Kevin must choose a major. Will it be Sleeping Around or Philosophy and Celibacy?

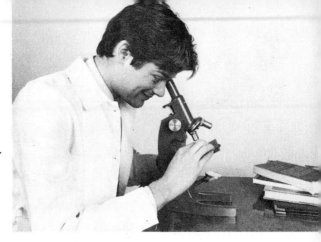

Year three and Kevin is off to India for his junior year abroad, where he teaches the sex-starved Indians a course in Intensive French Kissing.

His senior year, Kevin writes his thesis on sex as a means of transportation and stumbles upon a discovery: sex is also a means of reproduction! He publishes his findings, and his book becomes a national best seller. Kevin becomes a millionaire.

32. EVERY TIME A VIRGIN IS BORN, A PLANET REVERSES ITS ORBIT.

As a new virgin, you will notice remarkable changes in your entire being. Not only will your skin soften and your soul brighten, but you will find that you have a brand new zodiac sign: Virgo, the sign of the Virgin. Scientists are not sure why this happens, but many attribute it to planetary shift or to magic.

Virgo: The Woman. *Modest, knows how to say no, persuasive, fond of gardening but not of rakes, generous but not of herself, slow to anger but never gives in, aloof, gentle but firm if she doesn't want to do something. Her voice is as clear as a bell and her laugh brings joy to the world. Put on pedestal by men, never gets off.*

Virgo: The Male. *Strong, noble, disciplined, a defender of maidens, clean thoughts, doesn't rely on others for his own pleasure, knows how to say no. Well-clothed, self-respecting, cool-headed, well-mannered, knows how to deal with the aggression of others, kind to animals but is not one himself, attractive to women but not susceptible to flattery. Idolized by women.*

HOW TO FIND YOUR NEW BIRTHDAY

Old Birthday Sign	New Birthday	Old Birthday Sign	New Birthday
Aries (March 21–Apr 19). . .Sept 1		Libra (Sept 23–Oct 23) . . . .Sept 6	
Taurus (Apr 20–May 20) . . .Sept 2		Scorpio (Oct 24–Nov 21) . .Sept 7	
Gemini (May 21–June 21). .Sept 3		Sagittarius (Nov 22–Dec 21) Sept 8	
Cancer (June 22–July 22) . .Sept 4		Capricorn (Dec 22–Jan 19) Sept 9	
Leo (July 23–Aug 22) . . . . .Sept 5		Aquarius (Jan 20–Feb 18). .Sept 10	
Virgo (Aug 23–Sept 22) . . .(Aug 23 –Sept 22)		Pisces (Feb 19–March 20). .Sept 11	

33. 1983 TEST-TUBE BABIES RECALLED.

After being petitioned by the Center for Consumer Safety, General Baby opened a formal investigation of its 1981, 1982, and 1983 test-tube X-Baby models. A defect was found in one of the 1983 models, and 580,000 X-Babies were recalled.

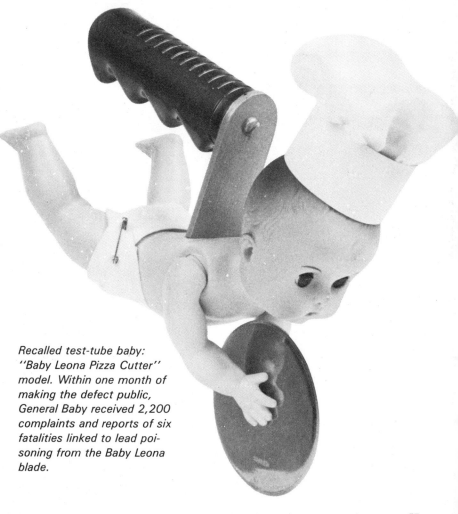

Recalled test-tube baby: "Baby Leona Pizza Cutter" model. Within one month of making the defect public, General Baby received 2,200 complaints and reports of six fatalities linked to lead poisoning from the Baby Leona blade.

34. HOW TO GIVE THE KISS OF DEATH.

Let's face it. A guy takes you out, say to a nice dinner and a play, maybe dancing . . . you owe him. If you are unable to pay him back monetarily, you must give of your body. A good-night kiss is a nice way of saying, "Thank you for spending a great deal of money on me." A good-night kiss does not say, "Why don't you come in and take off your clothes?" The kiss is not an invitation. It is a receipt for a lovely evening. Here's how to make sure your kiss is not a gateway to sex:

1. Stretch your lips to cover both your upper and lower sets of teeth. Now grip for dear life.

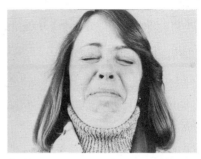

2. Close your eyes tightly as if you were in front of a firing squad.

3. Freeze. Pretend you stepped on a rusty nail a year ago and did not have a tetanus shot and the lockjaw you contracted just set in. *Never* open your mouth.

4. Prepare for the worst. When his lips touch your tightly sealed lips, count to three. Then back away decisively. He has had enough.

5. Using your whole arm, wipe the kiss from your mouth, making sure your date has seen you.

6. Give yourself a cootie shot and say good night.

35. CINDERELLA COMPLEX DEVELOPED IN HISTORIC PHILADELPHIA.

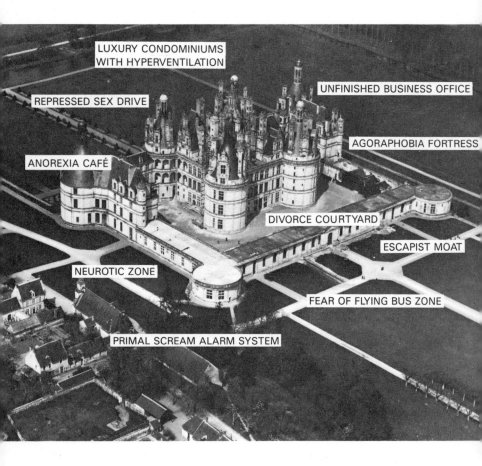

LUXURY CONDOMINIUMS WITH HYPERVENTILATION

UNFINISHED BUSINESS OFFICE

REPRESSED SEX DRIVE

AGORAPHOBIA FORTRESS

ANOREXIA CAFÉ

DIVORCE COURTYARD

ESCAPIST MOAT

NEUROTIC ZONE

FEAR OF FLYING BUS ZONE

PRIMAL SCREAM ALARM SYSTEM

37. YOUR DOODLES CAN BE SEXUALLY INTERPRETED.

1.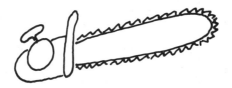

Interpretation: There is repressed tension between you and your partner.

2.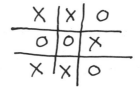

Interpretation: You are a kisser and a hugger.

3.

Interpretation: Your parents are having sexual problems.

4.

Interpretation: You are unbelievably miserable in your sexual life.

5.

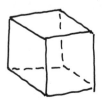

Interpretation: You are sick and should be locked up.

6.

Interpretation: Your wife is playing around with the milkman behind your back.

7.

Interpretation: You wish you could have sex with a spiral.

8.

Interpretation: You are a prude and a plagiarist.

37. THE PROFESSIONAL VIRGIN.
How to Pick Up Salad at a Singles Bar

Virgin Type C

HOW TO BECOME
THE PROFESSIONAL VIRGIN

1. Make sure no one can reach you by telephone before they speak to four different secretaries.

2. If you are meeting a man for lunch and he's late, record it on your time sheet and bill him accordingly.

3. Install a home computer in your bathtub so that you can work as you bathe.

4. Never talk to a man at work unless his office has a good view.

5. Go out only with men you can use as stepping stones on your way to the top.

38. IN THE YEAR 2000, CONTRACEPTIVES WILL BE SOLD IN VIDEO STORES.

Sex will continue to exist in the future, scientists predict, but there will be a few changes:

1. Most of the world's sex gadgets will be grown on the ocean floor.

2. With the aid of supersonic aerodynamics, you will be able to go from first base to third base in one millionth of a second.

3. Aphrodisiacs will have a vote in the U.N.

4. Foreplay will be computerized.

5. The Federal Reserve will determine the divorce rate and the supply of eligible men.

6. Boys and girls will no longer go "steady." They will go "constantly."

7. Women will no longer have miscarriages. They will have ms.carriages.

8. Bill Blass will introduce designer sex.

39. SEX-LINKED TRAITS ARE CARRIED BY WORMS IN THE HUMAN CELL.

Thanks to a new photo-nuclear microscope that magnifies 60 million times, it has become apparent that sex-linked traits formerly thought to be carried by chromosomes are actually carried by tiny, tiny worms living in human cells.

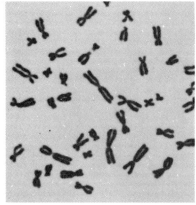

A photograph of so-called chromosomes (really worms) of a human female enlarged 60 million times.

THE STAGES OF MEIOSIS, THE PROCESS OF WORM DIVISION WITHIN THE HUMAN CELL

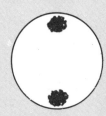

1. Before the music has begun at a boy/girl worm party.

2. Things begin to roll as the worms pair off.

3. Boys and girls go to opposite sides of the cell in preparation for Ladies Choice.

4. The girl worms lose their nerve and the worms remain divided.

40. ECONOMISTS FIND VIRGIN EMPLOYMENT RATE TRIPLES DUE TO AFFIRMATIVE ACTION PROGRAMS.

More than one hundred years ago, virgins were brought to this country to work the railway. They lived in squalid shanty towns and had to crack the ice in their washbowls each morning in order to wash their faces in the same water they had used to wash their dishes in the night before. Today, numerous careers are open to virgins — electrolysis, furniture restoration, and politics, to name a few. They've come a long way, but they still have a long way to go.

▶ Until 1951, virgins were required to sit in the back of the bus!

▶ In most states, it was also against the law to sell virgins cigarettes and liquor.

▶ Ronald Reagan was the first virgin ever elected president.

▶ Even today, most men would like a virgin but would not want their sisters to marry one.

41. HOW BABIES ARE MADE.

When gas is heated, it condenses, forming a very small fireball. As it grows hotter, the fireball continues to shrink until it finally explodes with a deafening roar scientists call "the big bang." After the dust settles, the obstetrician takes a rag and wipes off the baby that has been spontaneously created. Usually the baby stays in the hospital for a day or two to recover; it then goes home with a lady chosen to be its mother.

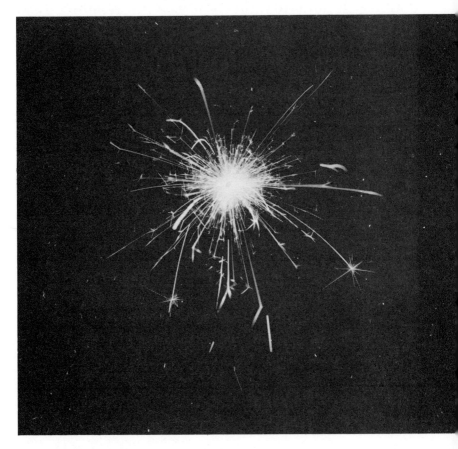

42. IN WALES, A WOMAN DIVORCES HER HUSBAND BY BARBECUING A ROASTED PIG ON A SPIT AND ROTATING IT THREE TIMES.

Not unlike the foods we eat and the climate we enjoy, the customs and mores of sex vary from country to country. In Rome, for instance, it is believed that drinking the water from the Fountain of Trevi is a foolproof contraceptive, while in Sweden, it is possible to have an abortion by mail. In Alaska, a woman—not unlike a polar bear—digs a hole in the snow in early winter and gives birth there a couple of months later.

43. MOST CARS HAVE HAD SOME KIND OF SEXUAL EXPERIENCE BEFORE THEY REACH 50,000 MILES.

The car, once thought to be an asexual organism, is now believed to have sexual feelings and patterns of behavior similar to those of human beings.

French cars are faster than American cars. Fifty percent of all Citroens manufactured today will go all the way before they reach twenty.

Mating dance of the automobile.

During the teen years, peer pressure forces cars to go "parking."

A 1955 Chevy hugs the road.

44. REPUTED AUTHOR OF BIBLE ADMITS: THE BIBLE READ BACKWARDS IS PORNOGRAPHIC AND WAS THE BASIS FOR THE MOVIE *EMMANUELLE.*

In this scene, the girls take off their bikini tops and go swimming in the pool.

45. WHAT TO DO IF YOU CAN'T LOCATE YOUR G SPOT.

Have a doorbell surgically implanted.

Finding your G-spot is not always easy.

46. WHICH ONE OF THESE IS NOT A SEX SYMBOL?

A.

B.

C.

D.

E.

F.

G.

H.

I.

47. SEX SYMBOLS CAUSE LAYERED HAIR.

The safety of your family, your children, and others dear to you may depend upon your recognizing sex symbols.

Officer Lamston says: "Know the Five Signs of the Sex Symbol."

1. A Sex Symbol chews gum loudly.

2. A Sex Symbol goes out with Andy Gibb or Loni Anderson.

3. A Sex Symbol has specials on TV.

4. A Sex Symbol has a real fur coat that looks like a fake fur coat.

5. A Sex Symbol is always jogging.

48. HOW TO TELL IF YOU'VE LOST YOUR VIRGINITY.

At last, the foolproof test:

1. When I pinch the skin on my forearm:
    a. I see an inch of fat.
    b. my lover rolls over in bed.
    c. my lover wants to have sex again.
    d. the baby cries.

2. My favorite activity is:
    a. anything under the covers with my lover.
    b. sleeping around.
    c. riding elevators.
    d. prostitution.

3. People tell me my best feature is:
    a. my willingness to give.
    b. my shiny hair.
    c. my bed.
    d. the curve of my cervix.

Answers: If your answers were 1(a), 2(c), and 3(b), you are a virgin. If they were not, you have lost your virginity. Find out who took it and ask for it back nicely.

49. WHY MEN CAN'T HAVE BABIES.

IT'S SIMPLE BIOLOGY:

Deep inside a man's stomach, there are many packages of little seeds. When a man kisses a woman he truly loves and is married to, a little seed that really wants to be born says, "Pick me!" This message is signaled to the brain, which relays it back to the stomach. If the brain says it's O.K., the seed travels up the stomach and through the mighty esophagus up to the man's mouth. When the man's lips touch the woman's, the little seed passes into the woman's mouth and down her mighty esophagus to her stomach, which is like a little garden, where the seed is planted. Every time the woman takes a drink, the seed is watered until one day it is big enough to be a baby. If a man and a woman do not want a baby, the woman takes an *oral contraceptive,* which blocks the passage in the mouth of this seed. Or she wears lipstick.

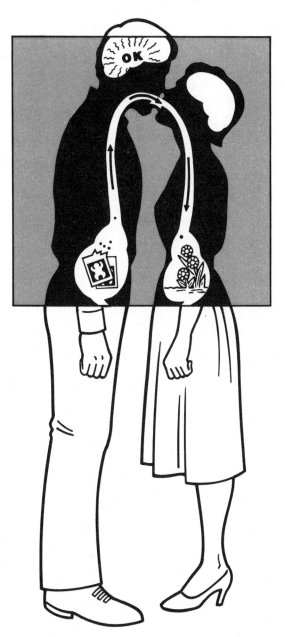

50. IN SCOTLAND, MEN HAVE BEEN TRYING TO HAVE BABIES FOR YEARS.

51. THE SOPHISTICATE VIRGIN.

Taking Off Her Gloves Could Lead to Sex

HOW TO BECOME
THE SOPHISTICATE VIRGIN

1. Never smile when the Viscount gives you his chalet in the hinterlands or he will think you think it is up to your standards.
2. Never finish your soufflé en croute or others will think you think the food is adequate.
3. Always leave the room when the bill arrives so others will think you are above money.
4. Never use an English word when a French word will confuse everyone.
5. Never breathe or others will think you are common.

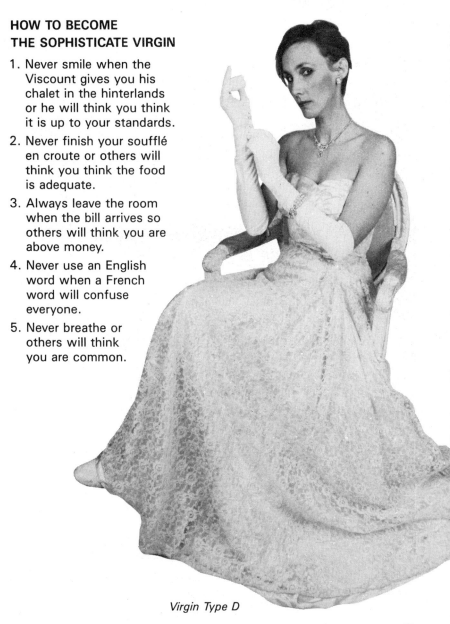

Virgin Type D

52. IN THE YEAR 2010, SEX WILL CONTINUE TO EXIST BUT YOU PROBABLY WILL NOT.

But just in case you survive:

1. There will be only four eligible men in the world: the prime minister of Japan, the first secretary of Russia, the secretary of defense of the United States, and a guy named Doug McGrath, who happened to be changing a fuse in the basement when the bomb fell.

2. You can tell if someone loves you by putting a Geiger counter to his or her heart.

3. Instead of saying it with flowers, sweethearts will say it with radioactive rubble.

4. Nude sunbathing will be a form of capital punishment.

5. Men and women will ozone layer their hair.

6. You will have to shoot your date if he or she tries to enter your fallout shelter.

53. IUD SPOTTED OVER ILLINOIS REGIONAL HIGH SCHOOL.

AP Jan. 12, 1983, Joliet, Ill.—Assertion that Mrs. Clarence Brown, aged 53, spotted IUD over "Honest Abe High" corroborated by photo Brown takes with Polaroid Swinger. "I never believed in that kind of stuff, but I saw the IUD with my own eyes. It looked like a giant Frisbee, all lit up. And I was the only one in town who didn't see *E.T.*!"

Actual photo of IUD.

54. NONEROGENOUS ZONES PINPOINTED.

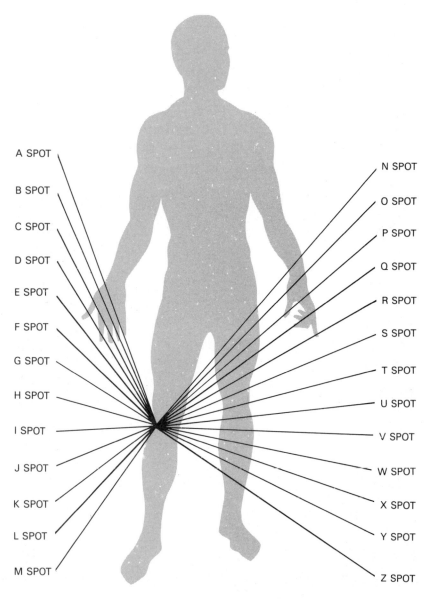

A SPOT
B SPOT
C SPOT
D SPOT
E SPOT
F SPOT
G SPOT
H SPOT
I SPOT
J SPOT
K SPOT
L SPOT
M SPOT

N SPOT
O SPOT
P SPOT
Q SPOT
R SPOT
S SPOT
T SPOT
U SPOT
V SPOT
W SPOT
X SPOT
Y SPOT
Z SPOT

FIGURE F

55. THE FEMINIST MOVEMENT HAS CHANGED THE BODY AS WELL AS THE FACE OF WOMANKIND.

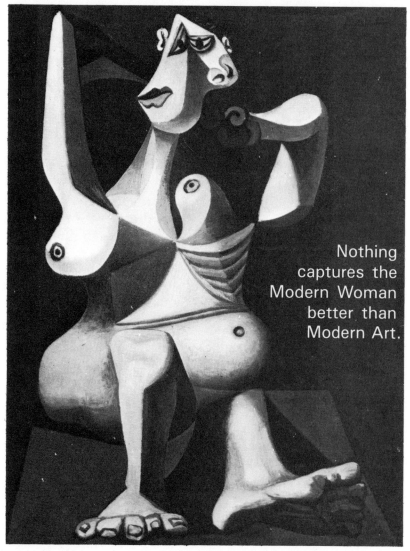

Nothing captures the Modern Woman better than Modern Art.

There are ten errors in this portrait of a woman. Can you spot them?

56. WHY YOU HAVE TO BE MARRIED TO HAVE A BABY.

You have to be married to have a baby because if you're not married, the man at the baby store won't give you one.

How does the man at the baby store know you're married?

It is easy to tell a married woman from an unmarried woman because a married woman is called "Mrs." and has the hairdo that mothers have.

Can you fake being married and fool the man at the baby store?

Yes, but only for a short while. If you are not married, an electronic buzzer will sound as you walk through the door with "your" new baby. This buzzer is similar to those used by department stores to prevent theft.

If you've gotten a baby from the baby store and you get divorced, can you get a refund?

No, but you can get a credit toward another baby *when* you are married again.

Do you have to have a very good marriage to have twins?

No, but you have to be a smart shopper and look for the sales. On certain days the baby store has special "Buy one get one free" deals.

Where does the man at the baby store get the babies?

When you are older, we will explain it to you.

57. HOW TO DECORATE YOUR G SPOT FOR UNDER $10,000.

Simply cut along the dotted line and move in. Ask your friends to help out with the heavier furniture.

58. POLYGA-ME, POLYGA-YOU! SEVEN NEW ALTERNATIVES TO MARRIAGE.

If a conventional marriage is not "your bag," may we suggest:

Bigamy—marrying another person while you are still married.

Pigamy—marrying a very short animal while you are still married.

Simonamy—having your car Simonized while you are still married.

Amyamy—marrying Amy while you are still married.

Tonsillectamy—having your tonsils out while you are still married.

Figamy—eating a fig while you are still married.

Origami—the Japanese art of folding paper into birds and flowers.

59. IF YOU HAVE A HISTORY OF VIRGINITY IN YOUR FAMILY, YOU ARE MORE LIKELY TO FIND YOURS.

Please help Barbara find her virginity.

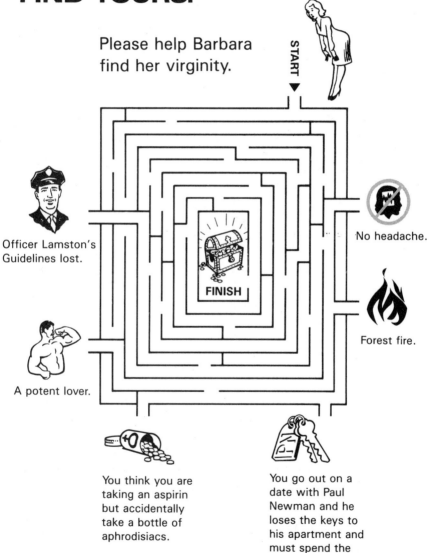

START ▼

Officer Lamston's Guidelines lost.

No headache.

Forest fire.

A potent lover.

FINISH

You think you are taking an aspirin but accidentally take a bottle of aphrodisiacs.

You go out on a date with Paul Newman and he loses the keys to his apartment and must spend the night at your place.

60. ANN LANDERS FINDS GIRLS WHO GO ALL THE WAY GET MORE MOSQUITO BITES.

Dear Ann,

I am in the ninth grade. Sam Johnson, who is cute, wants to carry my books home from school. If I let him, does this mean I'm a sex maniac?

Just Askin'

Dear Just Askin',

When it comes to sex, I think I'm just as "with it" as you can be. But when it comes to carrying books home from school, there's only one word for it: *immoral!!* Suppose you pass a motel on the way home from school? — Suppose Sam Johnson turns out to be a drug addict and he offers you a "cigarette"? Next thing you know, you're hooked! So next time Sam Johnson tries the old "Can I carry your books home" trick, ask yourself, "Is it worth it?"

* * * * * *

Dear Ann,

I am engaged to be married tomorrow but I don't know if I can go through with it. Last night my fiancé and I went all the way. We've been engaged for two years and I know he loves me. I can't believe I let this happen. I feel so guilty and ashamed. What should I do?

At the End of My Rope

Dear At,

You *should* be looking for a rope! You are a terrible, filthy person. You should kill yourself. The world would be well rid of you.

* * * * * *

Dear Ann,

My husband says he's found my G spot. I say he hasn't. Who's right?

In the Right

Dear In the Right,

Whenever boys and girls fight, all reason goes to the wind. But a word of advice: even if you know you're right, give in. Say something like, "Darling, you are so much smarter than I am and you are always right. Can I get you another helping of ravioli?" Don't worry about that G dot, whatever that is, just hold on to your man and thank the ever-lovin' Lord that you got him.

61. HOW BABIES ARE MADE.

Choose an extra grownup around the house you will not miss. (Make sure your grownup is not preshrunk.)

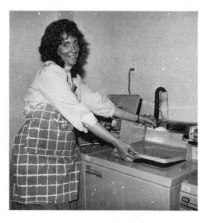

Put grownup in washing machine and set dial to Heavy Duty. Turn water to *hot.* Add one-half cup of detergent (or one cup if grownup is soiled). Add softener to final rinse.

Tumble dry grownup.

When you hear a little cry, open dryer immediately and take out your newborn baby — April fresh and static-free!

62. ONLY RECENTLY HAVE VIRGINS BEEN RECOGNIZED.

One of these women is a virgin.
Do you know which one?

63. BREAKING UP IS HARD TO DO.

Jean Harris's sex device.

64. POPULATION CONTROL EXPERTS FIND BOUILLON CUBE DISAPPOINTING AS CONTRACEPTIVE.

When the population of a small Asian country quadrupled last year, social scientists suspected that the massive administration of chicken-flavored bouillon cubes was not working as a birth control measure. The chief social worker at the Chicken Bouillon Clinic, however, was not prepared to rule conclusively that the cube per se was to blame, attributing the failure to the difficulty women have in following directions. Instead of dissolving the cube in one cup of boiling water as directed, women were seen in the rice paddies planting the cubes and then using the gold foil wrappers as money.

Research for a beef-flavored contraceptive for men was suspended at Unico Labs until more data is available.

While bouillon is still questionable as an effective means of birth control, scientists are heartened to find that in other areas, it is superior to the more conventional contraceptives.

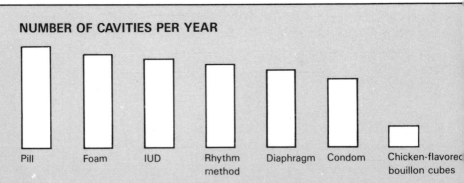

NUMBER OF CAVITIES PER YEAR

Pill Foam IUD Rhythm method Diaphragm Condom Chicken-flavored bouillon cubes

65. THE MARRIED VIRGIN.
Now with Self-Cleaning Uterus

**HOW TO BECOME
THE MARRIED VIRGIN**

1. Get married and have a few children.
2. Do your whole house over in Teflon.
3. Collect samples of cleaning products and compare them as to cost, use, and convenience.
4. When your husband sweeps you into his arms, straighten his tie.
5. Have a tantrum if someone doesn't shut the kitchen cabinets.

Virgin Type E

66. CHILDREN IN CALIFORNIA ARE 40 PERCENT OLDER THAN CHILDREN IN THE REST OF THE COUNTRY.

A face lift before ten years of age and a tax shelter before twelve is more the rule than the exception in affluent Beverly Hills. It is hardly surprising that it was here that the term *recreational sex* was coined.

LE SEX CAMP

- No swimming!
- No tennis!
- No hiking!
- No Indian names!
- NO SUPERVISION!
- No catalog. Just send money. Sex Camp, Box 1, Ely, KY.

Ad from the Los Angeles Times.

67. MISSING TEST-TUBE BABY FOUND: RAISED BY FAMILY OF LAB MICE.

It was more than thirteen years ago that the scientists at Unico Labs in St. Louis, Missouri, misplaced test-tube baby ''XY.'' Evidently the baby had crawled into an adjoining laboratory where white mice were being fed a diet consisting exclusively of saccharine and nicotine. Last week, Marlena Martin, the night cleaning woman at Unico Labs, discovered ''XY'' drinking Tab and smoking cigarettes with a gang of teenage mice, and immediately reported it to the police.

Caught in the act.

68. WHEN ZEBRAS GO ON DATES, THE GIRL ZEBRA ALWAYS BRINGS THE CORSAGE.

Girl zebras are known for their willingness to please their men. Here a girl zebra acts out her partner's favorite fantasy by dressing up as a barber pole while the boy zebra goes inside for a haircut.

69. HOW TO DETERMINE THE SEX OF YOUR CHILD... WITHOUT A DOCTOR!

Now you can determine the sex of your child without the risks of amnioscentesis. Here's a quick and safe test.

1. When my child asks to be excused at the restaurant to go to the bathroom, it goes into a door that looks like this:

(a)

```
┌─────────────┐
│             │
│   GENTS     │
│             │
│             │
│             │
│             │
│             │
└─────────────┘
```

(b)

```
┌─────────────┐
│             │
│   LADIES    │
│             │
│             │
│             │
│             │
│             │
└─────────────┘
```

The Results:
If you answered a, your child is a boy.
If you answered b, your child is a girl.
If you answered both a and b, you are wrong.

70. PLANTS IN FRANCE HAVE G SPOTS.

There are ten G spots in this picture. Can you find them?

71. VIRGINS RUN FASTER AND JUMP HIGHER THAN NONVIRGINS.

If you watch people who are virgins, no matter where they are—at home, in the street, at the beach—they handle themselves with beauty and grace. They radiate warmth and move easily, seeming to flow from room to room, place to place, area code to area code.

Virgins have happy marriages, successful careers, beautiful children, nice skin. They live longer, have better sex lives, and are better drivers. Virgins have it all.

Medical Facts

▶ Nonvirgins are twice as likely to get hives as virgins.

▶ Virgins are more able to withstand heat and cold.

▶ Virgins have an extra piece of cartilage in their legs that enables them to run faster and jump higher than non-virgins.

▶ Loss of virginity is accompanied by loss of hair.

72. FIRST TEST-TUBE MOTHER BORN IN CAMBRIDGE, MASSACHUSETTS.

Weighing in at 135 pounds, 3 ounces, Mrs. Edna Jones ("Mommy") was born on March 4, 1983, at 4 A.M. at the Boston Lying-In Hospital (hair: frosted blond). On March 5, she took her first step (toward Saks) and shortly thereafter, her first solid food (Ayds diet candy). On March 7 came "Mommy's" first words: "Andy Vandam's going to Harvard Business School and his SATs were lower than yours. Why can't you go to Harvard Business School?"

Mrs. Jones's Mommy Book *on display at the Houghton Library.*

73. SEX AT HIGH ALTITUDES: THE NEWEST CRAZE.

There is perhaps no greater thrill than getting to know someone under subzero temperatures and life-threatening circumstances. And you have a reasonable chance of surviving if you follow the rules.

THE SEX-AT-HIGH-ALTITUDE RULES

1. Choose a partner with a firm grip — someone who's insecure and will never "let go."
2. Wear at least three layers of clothing.
3. Set the oven 25 degrees lower.
4. The female always carries the oxygen tank.
5. Don't look down.

74. HOW BABIES ARE MADE.

Babies are made of thin layers of wood, called plies.

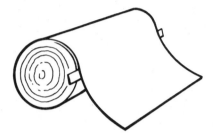

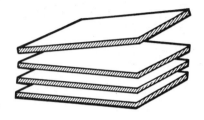

1. As the log turns, a sharp knife shaves off a thin sheet of wood.

2. Sheets of wood are glued together.

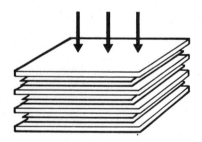

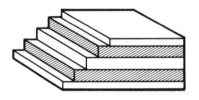

3. They are then squeezed together with great pressure.

4. Finally, they are polished with baby oil. This makes a baby smooth as silk.

75. FAKING PREGNANCY.

Why fake pregnancy? Aren't I only cheating myself?
It's all right to do it once and a while to keep your man happy. After all, he does a lot of things to give you pleasure. Besides, there are a lot of benefits to faking pregnancy.

What are the benefits of faking pregnancy?
1. No morning sickness.
2. You can eat anything you want whenever you want.
3. You can take off at least a week from work (with pay!).
4. You can get a seat on the bus.

Should I be doing exercises while I am faking pregnancy?
You should start exercising well *before* you even consider faking pregnancy. Your body will be undergoing enough changes without subjecting it to the added strain of muscle stress.

What foods should I eat to help me fake pregnancy?
Whole watermelons are excellent, as are whole hams. In general, eat in bulk and never chew. But remember, it is important to maintain a well-balanced diet when you're faking pregnancy.

Are there dangers to faking pregnancy?
Before modern medicine, many women suffered the loss of their lives, but today, the mortality rate is negligible. If there are problems during ''delivery'' and the doctor asks you whether he should save the baby or the mother, always go for the mother.

76. HOW MEN FAKE PREGNANCY.

Four Easy Steps

1. When you go to take the rabbit test, make sure to bring a cribsheet.

2. Have your best friend surprise you with a baby shower.

3. Never give up your seat on the bus.

4. When you come out of the delivery room and your wife asks you where the baby is, say, ''I thought you had it!''

77. THE LIBRARIAN VIRGIN.
Nine Out of Ten Prefer the Missionary to the Missionary Position

**HOW TO BECOME
THE LIBRARIAN VIRGIN**

1. Suck three lemons a day.
2. Scowl at anyone who raises his voice above a whisper.
3. Learn to eat saltines as if you have no teeth.
4. If you have to have lunch with a family friend and he is late, fine him twenty-five cents.
5. Be able to identify the following leathers used on books: calfskin, seal, pigskin, Moroccan, and Russian.

Virgin Type F

78. FACTS OF LIFE DISPROVED.

Sexologists at the Lite Sex Clinic have recently disclosed that the heretofore undisputed "Facts of Life" theory—that through sexual activity, offspring can be produced—is entirely fallacious. The real Facts of Life, as endorsed by the Lite Sex Clinic, are as follows:

1. You can never have too many glasses.

2. English accents make you sound more intelligent.

3. No one ever reads footnotes.

4. When things go well, you always get a migraine headache.

5. Whenever you think things can't get worse, they do.

6. It takes one to know one.

79. VIRGINITY HAS MORE USES THAN THE SOYBEAN.

AS AN EASY WAY TO GET
A GOOD CREDIT RATING.

AS AN EXCELLENT WALL HANGING
FOR OFFICES AND HOMES.

AS A MEANS OF
MONETARY EXCHANGE.

AS A SACRIFICE
TO APPEASE THE GODS.

PLASTICS.

80. LEON TROTSKY WAS THE FOUNDER OF SOCIAL KISSING.

Many have claimed to be the originators of social kissing, but a close study of Leon Trotsky's life proves conclusively that the founder of socialism was also the founder of social kissing.

Leon Trotsky demonstrates the social kissing technique he made famous.

THE LIFE OF LEON TROTSKY

1895: Trotsky becomes a Populist and discovers that kissing babies makes you popular.

1898: Trotsky becomes an active Socialist and has to attend a lot of parties. By accident, he greets a woman he doesn't know with a kiss. Other guests follow his lead. A fad has begun.

1902: After his escape from Siberia, Trotsky works in London with Lenin on a revolutionary journal. He is introduced to the world of publishing and teaches the people he meets how to kiss people you don't even know. His teachings become known throughout the land.

1905–1917: Trotsky travels to Paris, Switzerland, New York, and Siberia, where he spreads the word. Trotsky's dream of social kissing as an international movement is finally realized.

1917: During his term as People's Commissar under Lenin, Trotsky revolutionizes the social kiss by adding the social hug.

1940: Trotsky is axed to death.

81. SEX IS NOT CONTAGIOUS.

It is hereditary.

82. IN OTHER COUNTRIES, THEY ORDER BABIES FROM A CATALOG.

How babies are delivered around the world

New equipment allows babies to be stacked and stored in the Tokyo General Post Office.

Perplexed Israeli postman: this special delivery baby was sent to "No Such Address."

Babies "shooting the chutes" in a German post office.

Donkeys still carry babies overland in Mexico.

83. HOW TO TELL IF YOUR MARRIAGE WILL SURVIVE.

$$\frac{h + w + y}{6} + 1 = n$$

Let h = your height (without shoes)

Let w = your weight

Let y = the number of years you have been married

If n is an even number, your marriage will survive.

If n is an odd number, your marriage will end in tragic divorce.

84. NO TWO SNOWFLAKES HAVE EVER BEEN MARRIED FOR OVER THREE YEARS!

CAUSES OF DIVORCE AMONG AMERICAN SNOWFLAKES.

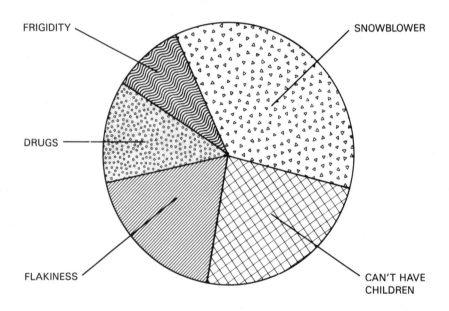

FRIGIDITY

SNOWBLOWER

DRUGS

FLAKINESS

CAN'T HAVE CHILDREN

85. HOW BABIES ARE MADE.

June crop is dusted with baby powder.

86. HOW BABIES GROW.

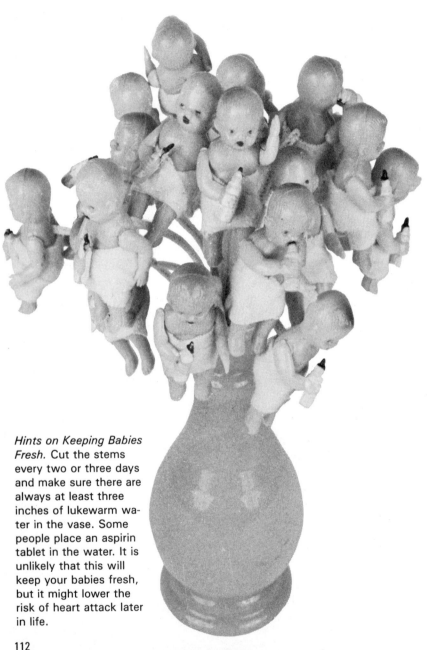

Hints on Keeping Babies Fresh. Cut the stems every two or three days and make sure there are always at least three inches of lukewarm water in the vase. Some people place an aspirin tablet in the water. It is unlikely that this will keep your babies fresh, but it might lower the risk of heart attack later in life.

87. THE TEASE VIRGIN.
Not As Advertised

**HOW TO BECOME
THE TEASE VIRGIN**

1. Advertise in the personal column for a date for Saturday night.
2. When your first customer calls, invite him over to your house for an intimate dinner.
3. Before he arrives, fluff the pillows and dim the lights.
4. When he shows up, ask him if he has to get up early in the morning.
5. After dinner, when he makes a pass, slap his face and make a citizen's arrest.

Virgin Type G

88. TRAINING BRA READY FOR THE 1988 OLYMPICS.

Playtex announced recently that its training bra, ''Littlest Angel,'' will be entering the 1988 Olympics. The bra will be the first undergarment in history to enter a world sports competition.

''Littlest Angel'' finishes the 200-meter breast stroke in perfect form.

89. HOW TO BE MORE SEXUALLY AGGRESSIVE.

1. Donna arrives at the party and takes a look around. Spotting Rich, a cute guy, Donna makes her first move. She lifts her right leg and pushes off from her left, lifting her arms in position for the thrust forward.

2. An obstacle in her path. Donna looks like she might surmount it as she hurls herself forward. Her timing is excellent. Rich has just broken up with his fiancée, Gwen.

3. Donna arrives at Rich's feet, gently invading his space. Watch out, Rich!

90. DATING YOUR GYNECOLOGIST

"Take off your clothes, Linda," said Dr. Dansey.

"I don't do that kind of thing on a first date, Doctor," Linda replied.

So Shirley, Dr. Dansey's secretary, made an appointment for another date.

"I really liked your Pap smear, Linda."

"Oh, it was nothing."

"The Good'n'Plenty looks good," said Dr. Dansey.

"Make that two," piped in Linda.

"How was your day?"
Linda asked the gynecologist.

"Very busy. Fortunately,
Mrs. Harold Cluney canceled
her 12:15. Do you know
her? . . ."

Dr. Dansey and Linda
watch the movie for a
while.

"She's barren as a rock,"
said Dr. Dansey.

"Thank you, Dr. Dansey,
for the lovely time."

"See you in six months, Linda."

*From Dansey, Milton G., "Photo-
synthesis and Human Reproduction,"
Journal of American Medicine,
April 3, 1983.

91. CURE FOR SPURNED LOVERS.

Broken heart surgery.

92. WOMEN WHO DO NOT WISH TO BE REGARDED AS SEX OBJECTS HAVE FEWER DATES ACCORDING TO *SHE!* MAGAZINE SURVEY.

There are eight sex objects in this picture. Try and locate them.

93. G SPOTS MUST BE VIEWED THROUGH DARK GLASS OR BLINDNESS WILL RESULT.

In Bar Harbor, Maine, a woman by the name of Mrs. Florence Anderson has a G spot so brilliant, it is used by sailors who are lost in the fog. Were it not for Mrs. Anderson, twelve sailors would have tragically lost their lives during Hurricane Bess.

94. HOW TO RECOGNIZE A BOY VIRGIN.

He talks about sex all the time.

95. PHYSIOLOGICAL THEORY OF LOVE REFUTED.

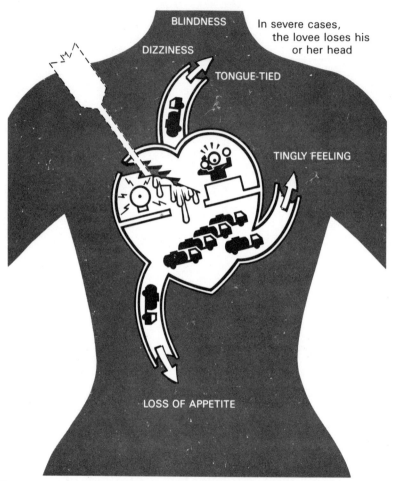

BLINDNESS

DIZZINESS

TONGUE-TIED

In severe cases, the lovee loses his or her head

TINGLY FEELING

LOSS OF APPETITE

The lover shoots an invisible arrow into the heart of the lovee. When the arrow pierces the heart, the heart breaks and the chemicals that were stored within the heart's cavity seep through the crack, causing the heart to ache and pulsate. This activates an alarm system that sends a truck dispatcher—who resides in the upper auricles—into action. The truck dispatcher alerts his truckers to disseminate the spilled chemicals throughout the body, which brings on the symptoms of love. The chemical attraction between the lover and lovee is complete.

Disproof: There is absolutely no way that an entire truck could fit through the aorta, which is no wider than a common drinking straw.

96. NEW PHYSIOLOGICAL THEORY OF LOVE.

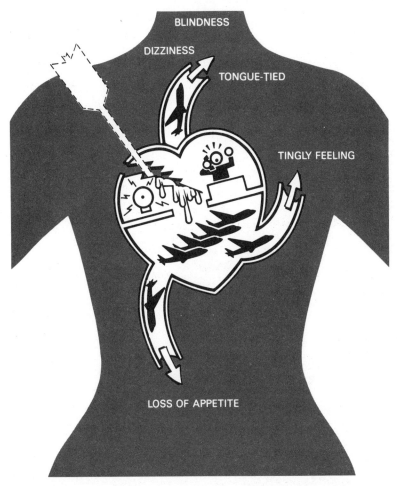

Contrary to popular belief, the chemicals of love are carried not by truck but by Boeing 747 jet airplanes.

97. NEW VIRUS CAUSES MEANINGFUL RELATIONSHIPS.

A new virus has been created at Unico Labs that researchers hope will help individuals who are unable to sustain meaningful relationships. The virus, dubbed "the caring virus," has been injected into the bloodstreams of a hundred callous human subjects with positive effects. Unico plans to spread the virus in 1990.

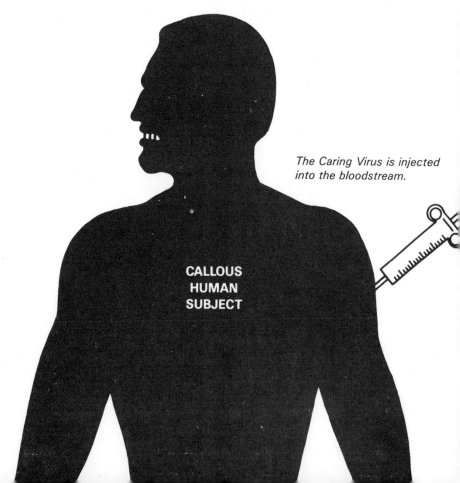

The Caring Virus is injected into the bloodstream.

CALLOUS
HUMAN
SUBJECT

1. After the Caring Virus is injected into the bloodstream, it attaches itself to a Selfish Cell.

2. After the Caring Virus has shot its nucleic acid through the Selfish Cell wall, it forces the Selfish host cell to make copies of it.

3. The Caring Virus then forces the Selfish Cell to destroy itself.

4. By this time, the antibodies of Cynicism and Distrust have rallied. They bombard the Caring Virus.

5. But the Caring Virus is so strong, it defeats the antibodies, who retreat.

98. IF YOUR VIRGINITY IS LOST AND NOT FOUND WITHIN THE FISCAL YEAR, YOU MAY USE IT AS A TAX WRITE-OFF.

Since the days of the New Deal, the government has been more sympathetic to "the little guy." Here, Tom enlists the help of the U.S. Air Force to help him locate his missing virginity. They are glad to lend Tom a hand, even though it means parachuting into a raging forest fire.

99. HOW TO TELL IF YOUR WIFE IS A VIRGIN.

While your wife is sleeping, insert a pea and nine mattresses beneath her. Then keep a close watch. By the end of the night, you will know whether the woman you've loved and cherished for so many years is a virgin.

The Pea Test

Virgin

Virgin

Virgin

Virgin Mother

100. NEW SEX LEGISLATION.

Our democracy is always working. As the lifestyles of American men and women change, our laws change to meet them.

▶ In Pennsylvania, the Department of Transportation has issued an ordinance stating that anyone who intends to have a sex-change operation must notify the Registry of Motor Vehicles of said change within sixty days or his/her license will be revoked and he/she will be required to attend twelve hours of driver's education classes before obtaining a new license.

▶ If a surrogate mother in Louisiana decides to keep her baby, she must appear before a surrogate judge.

▶ In Illinois, the ground-breaking state in palimony law, if you share the same cab on the way back from O'Hare Airport with a member of the opposite sex and your "partner" is smoking a cigarette and you say, "Gee, what if there were diet cigarettes" and he/she later becomes a diet cigarette mogul, you are legally entitled to half of his/her yearly income.

▶ If you sell a contraceptive to someone in New Mexico while he/she is extracting anthracite from the earth, you will be fined $300 for corrupting a miner.

▶ In Seattle, there are no-fault abortions for Catholics who wish to be forgiven.

▶ Pregnant women in California who do not practice their Jane Fonda Pregnancy Exercises are served with malpractice suits.